To Colin + Evan
Happy Easter 1990.

To Colin + Evan
Happy Easter 1990.

ISBN 0–8317–8026–6
Copyright © 1989 Victoria House Publishing Ltd, Bath, England.
Adapted from the Gospels.
This edition published 1989 by Gallery Books, an imprint of
W.H. Smith Publishers, Inc., 112 Madison Avenue, New York,
New York, 10016.
Printed in Italy.

Gallery Books are available for bulk purchase
for sales promotions and premium use. For
details write or telephone the Manager of
Special Sales, W.H. Smith Publishers, Inc.,
112 Madison Avenue, New York, New York.
(212) 532-6600.

The Story of Easter

Adapted by Andrew Langley

Illustrated by Chris Rothero

GALLERY BOOKS
An Imprint of W. H. Smith Publishers Inc.
112 Madison Avenue
New York City 10016

Jesus was the Son of God, and long ago God sent him down from Heaven to be born as a little boy and to grow up as a man on Earth. Jesus knew that he had been sent to Earth to teach the word of God and to die for the sins of all the people in the world. Because of his life and death on Earth, many people would come to believe in God's goodness. When Jesus grew up, he preached God's word, and performed many wonderful miracles. He gathered twelve disciples to help him in his work.

One day Jesus traveled to Jerusalem. As he approached the town, Jesus sent two of his disciples ahead, telling them that they would find a donkey tethered in the street. They found the donkey as Jesus had said they would. Jesus mounted the donkey, and rode it into the city, where crowds rushed out to greet him, cheering and waving. They threw down cloaks and palm branches for him to ride over.

When Jesus arrived at the temple in Jerusalem, he saw that merchants and money-lenders were using the courtyard for business. He grew angry and drove them away, pushing over their tables and stalls. "God's house is a house of prayer!" he cried. "You have turned it into a den of thieves!" Jesus taught in the temple every day, and many people came to hear him. The temple priests were jealous, and decided secretly that he must die.

When the day of the Passover feast came, Jesus and his disciples sat down and ate their supper together. During the meal Jesus took a loaf of bread and gave pieces to each of the disciples. "Take this," he said. "This is my body." Then he gave them each a sip of wine and said, "This is my blood." But Jesus knew that this was the last meal he would share with his disciples.

"There is someone sitting at this table who is going to betray me," he said. The disciples were very upset, and they all denied that they would betray Jesus. One disciple asked Jesus who it was. Jesus replied. "I will give this piece of bread to the one who is going to betray me," and he handed the bread to Judas.

After supper Jesus and his disciples walked to a garden called Gethsemane, on the Mount of Olives. He told most of his disciples to sit and wait for him. Then he went further on, with three of them. He asked these three to stay awake nearby, while he prayed alone. When he knelt down to pray he was overwhelmed with sadness, but he told God that he was ready to face death.

Suddenly a crowd of soldiers and priests burst into the garden. They were led by the traitor, Judas, who came up to Jesus and kissed him on the cheek. This was a sign to the soldiers to take hold of Jesus and lead him to the house of the High Priest, Caiaphas, who wanted him to die.

Jesus was taken to the palace to appear before Pontius Pilate, the Roman governor. Pilate turned Jesus over to his enemies, and he was condemned to death. His guards gave him a robe to wear and put a crown of thorns on his head and laughingly called him 'King of the Jews'. They made him carry a heavy wooden cross and drove him through the busy streets of Jerusalem.

Jesus was led to a place called Golgotha, on a hill outside the city. There the soldiers nailed him to the cross. Many people gathered round to watch, and amongst the crowd were Mary, his mother, and his disciple John. They stood silently beneath the cross, and, after many hours, Jesus died.

Friends of Jesus took his body down from the cross. They wrapped it in clean linen cloth and carried it to a nearby tomb cut out of rock. They laid Jesus gently in the tomb, and then they rolled a big stone securely across the entrance. Soldiers were ordered to stand on guard outside, in case any of the disciples tried to steal the body.

Two days later, just after sunrise, Mary Magdalene came to look at the tomb. She saw that the stone had been rolled away from the entrance. She looked inside and saw that the tomb was empty. In panic, Mary rushed to get some of the disciples. When they arrived at the tomb, they also saw that Jesus' body was gone. He had risen from the dead!

After he had risen, Jesus spent forty days and nights on Earth. He first appeared to Mary Magdalene, but the disciples did not believe her until they saw Jesus for themselves. He appeared amongst them several times, and on his final visit he blessed them all, and said: "Go out to every part of the world. Tell everyone that God will forgive their sins."

Then Jesus walked away from the disciples, and was carried up to Heaven. One day soon afterwards, the disciples were praying together and talking of Jesus. Suddenly the whole room was filled with a roaring sound. Tongues of fire appeared and settled on each of the disciples. They felt filled with God's power, and ran out into the street, full of happiness. They began to tell everyone about Jesus, and soon converted many people to Christianity.

People all over the world still celebrate Jesus' return to life. Easter Sunday is the day he is believed to have risen from the dead. It takes place in springtime, a season when new life starts to appear after the long winter. Young animals are born, new leaves and flowers grow, and the Earth becomes warmer again. It is a time for looking forward to the future with hope.